# WISDOM AND QUOTES

# FROM

# EAST AND WEST

Compiled by

P. S. Verma

Published by Kindle Publishing,
United States of America

www.amazon.com

ISBN 9798673097014

TO MY FAMILY

# TABLE OF CONTENTS

# **INTRODUCTION**

This is my humble attempt to pass on wisdom and notable quotes from both the orient and occident. A few of them may not represent wise thoughts, but still convey strong messages in a humorous way. The scope is endless. I have attempted to include whatever touched my heart during my interactions with good people or reading good books and articles over the last several years. While it is impossible to replace the importance of reading good books (which offer more precise contexts and situations), it becomes imperative on my part to convey the "real message" hidden in the original prose or verse.

Most of the quotes written originally in English are self-explanatory; however, when they are translated from another language into English, it becomes difficult to transfer their humor, essence, and brilliance. Every language has its own beauty and splendor and is associated with its own culture. Poems and verses have their own way of revealing messages sometimes difficult to understand (even by those who know that very language). So rather than a word-by-word translation, I have attempted to convey the "feelings" expressed in other languages as I understood them, into English.

When I was growing up in India, most of the verses (in Hindi or Sanskrit) included here were part of textbooks in elementary and middle schools. They provided great moorings in culture, and a moral compass for the rest of life. I still remember many of them. However, such words of wisdom are not taught in India anymore on the name of secularism, even though many of those verses were written by Muslim saints like Kabir and Rahim. Their teachings and quotes were rooted in the eastern culture and *Sanatana Dharma*.

All of the quotes from intellectuals, saints, sages, poets, and famous figures are put together here in the hope that one will contemplate and reflect on these quotes...some philosophical, some motivational, some funny, and others useful in everyday life. It is also hoped that readers, in the East or West, who have forgotten or were never exposed to these pearls before, will derive some practical meaning and use in life.

The quotes are not arranged in any order of subject or author. However, at the beginning of the book, I did group some wise words of Acharya Chanakya, taken from his writing, as they belong to a very special category of being practical, blunt and direct, socially useful, and yet intellectually rich.

Acharya Chanakya (370 - 283 BCE) was one of the most famous and popular historical figures in India. He was a master of wise counsel and diplomacy, along with a great scholar, strategist, writer, and professor of Economics and Political Science. He taught at Takshasila University, the oldest known university in the world (founded circa 800 BCE). Chanakya was also the author of the book Arthashastra (Economics); his work was lost until an original copy was discovered in India in 1915. Chanakya was a great strategist and his work predates Machiavelli's by about 1800 years. After Alexander the Great's death, Salukis commanded Alexander's massive army to invade India. Chanakya, also known as Kautilya or Vishnugupta, single-handedly masterminded the Chandragupta Empire's victory over

Alexander's army, in which Salukis was taken a prisoner. During this period, the borders of the Chandragupta Empire extended far beyond those of modern India. Chanakya teachings are still relevant 2300 years later.

# QUOTES AND WORDS OF WISDOM

1.  "An egoist can be won over by being respected, a crazy person can be won over by allowing him to behave in an insane manner and a wise person can be won over by truth." - <u>Acharya Chanakya (370-283 BCE)</u>

2.  "When your enemy is making mistakes, don't interrupt him." - <u>Acharya Chanakya</u>

3.  "As soon as fear approaches near, attack and destroy it." - <u>Acharya Chanakya</u>

4.  "A human being should strive for four things in life - duty, money, happiness, and salvation. A person who hasn't striven for even one of these things has wasted life." - <u>Acharya Chanakya</u>

5. "Do not reveal what you have thought upon doing, but by wise council keep it secret being determined to carry it into execution." - <u>Acharya Chanakya</u>

6. "It is better to die than to preserve this life by incurring disgrace. The loss of life causes a moment's grief, but disgrace brings grief every day of one's life." - <u>Acharya Chanakya</u>

7. "There is no austerity equal to a balanced mind, and there is no happiness equal to contentment; there is no disease like covetousness, and no virtue like mercy." - <u>Acharya Chanakya</u>

8. "The biggest *guru-mantra* is to never share your secrets with anybody. It will destroy you. If you cannot keep your secrets with you then how can you trust others to keep them secret?" - <u>Acharya Chanakya</u>

9.  "A person should not be too honest. Straight trees in the forest are cut first, and honest people are screwed first." - Acharya Chanakya

10.  "The earth is supported by the power of truth; it is the power of truth that makes the sun shine and the winds blow; indeed, all things rest upon truth." - Acharya Chanakya

11.  "Books are as useful to a stupid person as a mirror is useful to a blind person." - Acharya Chanakya

12.  "Education is one's best friend. An educated person is respected everywhere. Education beats both beauty and youth." - Acharya Chanakya

13.  "Even if a snake is not poisonous, it should pretend to be venomous." - Acharya Chanakya

14.  "He who befriends a man whose conduct is vicious, whose vision impure, and who is notoriously crooked, is rapidly ruined." - Acharya Chanakya

15.  "If you get to learn something even from the worst of creatures, don't hesitate." - Acharya Chanakya

16.  "In a state where the ruler lives like a common man, the citizens live like kings. And in the state where the ruler lives like a king, the citizens live like beggars." - Acharya Chanakya

17.  "Jealousy is another name for failure." - Acharya Chanakya

18.  "Never make friends with people who are above or below you in status. Such friendships will never give you any happiness." - Acharya Chanakya

19. "One who is in search of knowledge should give up the search of pleasure, and one who is in search of pleasure should give up the search of knowledge." - <u>Acharya Chanakya</u>

20. "The four greatest enemies of a man are - the father who has taken a loan, the characterless mother, the beautiful but promiscuous wife and the stupid child." - <u>Acharya Chanakya</u>

21. "The world's biggest power is the youth and beauty of a woman." - <u>Acharya Chanakya</u>

22. "There is some self-interest behind every friendship. There is no friendship without self-interests. This is a bitter truth." - <u>Acharya Chanakya</u>

23. "Treat your kid like a darling for the first five years. For the next ten years, admonish them strictly. By the time they turn sixteen, treat them like a

friend. Your grown-up children are your best friends." - <u>Acharya Chanakya</u>

24.  "The wise man should never go into a country where there are no means of earning one's livelihood, where the people have no dread of anybody, have no sense of shame, no intelligence, or a charitable disposition." - <u>Acharya Chanakya</u>

25.  "O wise man! Give your wealth only to the worthy and never to others. The water of the sea received by the clouds is always sweet." - <u>Acharya Chanakya</u>

26.  "He who is overly attached to his family members experiences fear and sorrow, for the root of all grief is attachment. Thus, one should discard attachment to be happy." - <u>Acharya Chanakya</u>

27. "Purity of speech, of the mind, of the senses, and of a compassionate heart are needed by one who desires to rise to the divine platform." - <u>Acharya Chanakya</u>

28. "A man is great by deeds, not by birth." - <u>Acharya Chanakya</u>

29. "Those who have consideration for others have their problems solved or destroyed automatically, and they receive (unseen) benefits at every step." - <u>Acharya Chanakya</u> (This is similar to what Yudhishthira said in *Mahabharat* that if you aim at another's benefit, your own selfish end would also be served in the process.)

30. "There is no present or future for a lazy person." - <u>Acharya Chanakya</u>

31. "The absence of enthusiasm ruins even his own fortune bestowed by God." - <u>Acharya Chanakya</u>

32. "Every relationship is linked with some common advantage to be achieved." - <u>Acharya Chanakya</u>

33. "No advice should be given to vile persons. Therefore, such persons should never be relied upon." - <u>Acharya Chanakya</u>

34. "A frugal diet is the key to good health." - <u>Acharya Chanakya</u>

35. "One must follow one's *Dharma* [a set of eternal principles commonly confused as *religion*] in this world. Even the ghosts and spirits follow their own Dharma. The birthplace of Dharma is compassion. An honest donation is the root of Dharma. He who follows his Dharma truthfully

scores victory in all his worldly endeavors." - <u>Acharya Chanakya</u>

36. "Never go on a long journey alone." - <u>Acharya Chanakya</u>

37. "There is no place except hell for an ungrateful person." - <u>Acharya Chanakya</u>

38. "One's tongue (speech) can be the source of poison or nectar." - <u>Acharya Chanakya</u>

39. "One reaps as one sows. "(यथा बीजं तथा निष्पत्तिः)" - <u>Acharya Chanakya</u>

40. "The impatient persons have no present or future." - <u>Acharya Chanakya</u>

41. "The history of humanity is the history of only a few men. Do not be a sheep, you are a lion." - <u>Swami Vivekanand (1863-1902)</u>

42.  "I find that the harder I work, the more luck I seem to have." - <u>Thomas Jefferson (1743-1826), 3rd President of the United States</u>

43.  "Good people do not need laws to tell them to act responsibly, while bad people will find a way around the laws." - <u>Plato (427-347 B.C.)</u>

44.  "The difference between 'involvement' and 'commitment' is like an eggs-and-ham breakfast: the chicken was 'involved' - the pig was 'committed'." - <u>Unknown</u>

45.  "If you are going through hell, keep going." - <u>Winston Churchill (1874-1965)</u>

46.  "The significant problems we face cannot be solved at the same level of

thinking we were at when we created them." - <u>Albert Einstein (1879-1955)</u>

47. "First they ignore you, then they laugh at you, then they fight you, then you win." - <u>Gandhi (1869-1948)</u>

48. "I would have made a good Pope." - <u>The disgraced US President Richard M. Nixon (1913-1994)</u>

49. "Anything that is too stupid to be spoken is sung." - <u>Voltaire (1694-1778)</u>

50. "Few things are harder to put up with than a good example." - <u>Mark Twain (1835-1910)</u>

51. "Men have become the tools of their tools." - <u>Henry David Thoreau (1817-1862)</u>

52. "I think it would be a good idea." - <u>Gandhi on 'what he thought of Western civilization'</u>

53.  "No matter how great a man, don't follow him blindly." - <u>Swami Vivekanand</u>

54.  "Remember, this world is very old; it was not created only two or three thousand years ago. It is taught here in the West that the society began eighteen hundred years ago, with the New Testament. Before that there was no society. That may be true with regard to the West, but it is not true as regards the whole World." - <u>Swami Vivekanand, in a lecture delivered in Los Angeles, CA in 1900 CE.</u>

55.  "There is no reason anyone would want a computer in their home." - <u>Ken Olson, president, chairman and founder of Digital Equipment Corp., 1977</u>

56.  "The concept is interesting and well-formed, but in order to earn better

than a 'C', the idea must be feasible." - A Yale University management professor in response to student Fred Smith's paper proposing reliable overnight delivery service. Smith went on to found Federal Express Corp.

57.  "Everything that can be invented has been invented." - Charles H. Duell, Commissioner, U.S. Office of Patents, 1899

58.  "There are only two ways to live your life. One is as though nothing is a miracle. The other is as though everything is a miracle." - Albert Einstein (1879-1955)

59.  "The quality of your life depends on the quality of your attention." - Deepak Chopra

60.  "The worst lie that you ever tell yourself is that you were born a sinner or a wicked man. He alone is a sinner

who sees a sinner in another man." - <u>Swami Vivekanand, in New York (on Christian doctrine that we are all born sinners)</u>

61.  "Ask nothing; want nothing in return. Give what you have to give; it will come back to you - but do not think of that now, it will come back multiplied a thousand-fold - but the attention must not be on that. Yet have the power to give: give and there it ends." - <u>Swami Vivekanand in Los Angeles, 1900</u>

62.  "Whether you will it or not, you have to give. The moment you say, 'I will not', the blow comes; you are hurt." - <u>Swami Vivekanand</u>

63.  "The man who has control over his own mind assuredly will have control over every other mind. That is why purity and morality have been always the object of religion; a pure, moral

man has control of himself." - <u>Swami Vivekanand in Los Angeles, 1900</u>

64. "Breathing and posturing, etc. no doubt help in Yoga, but they are merely physical. The great preparations are mental. The first thing necessary is a quiet and peaceable life." - <u>Swami Vivekanand in Los Angeles</u>

65. "He who desires a comfortable and nice life, and at the same time wants to realize the self, is like a fool who, wanting to cross the river, caught hold of a crocodile, mistaking it for a log of wood." - <u>Swami Vivekanand in Los Angeles</u>

66. "Clothes make a man." - <u>Mark Twain</u>

67. "Do not sleep with your head pointing northward or westward." - <u>An old Indian Proverb</u>

68. "When the missionaries arrived, the Africans had the land and the missionaries had the Bible. They taught us to pray with our eyes closed. When we opened them, they had the land and we had the Bible." - Jomo Kenyatta (1889-1978), President and Founding Father of Kenya in *Absurdities in the name of Religion*

69. "Hinduism.....gave itself no name, because it set itself no sectarian limits; it claimed no universal adhesion, asserted no sole infallible dogma, set up no single narrow path or gate of salvation; it was less a creed or cult than a continuously enlarging tradition of the God-ward endeavor of the human spirit. An immense many-sided and many staged provision for a spiritual self-building and self-finding, it had some right to speak of itself by the only name it knew, the eternal religion, Santana Dharma...." - Sri Aurobindo (1872-1950)

70. "The Hindu religion is the only one of the world's great faiths dedicated to the idea that the Cosmos itself undergoes an immense, indeed an infinite, number of deaths and rebirths. It is the only religion in which the time scales correspond, to those of modern scientific cosmology." - <u>Carl Sagan (1934-1996), Astrophysicist and Professor at Cornell University</u>

71. "Shed the burden of judgment - you will feel much lighter." - <u>Deepak Chopra</u>

72. "Once a person has faith, he has achieved everything. There is nothing greater than faith." - <u>Sri Ramakrishna (1836-1886)</u>

73. "One should not be ashamed of chanting God's holy name. One does not succeed so long as one has these three: shame, hatred, and fear." - <u>Sri Ramakrishna</u>

74. "If a man repeats the name of God, his body, mind, and everything become pure. Why should one talk only about sin and hell, and such things? Say but once, *'O Lord, I have undoubtedly done wicked things, but I won't repeat them.'* And have faith in His name." - <u>Sri Ramakrishna</u>

75. "The man who does not read good books has no advantage over the man who cannot read them." - <u>Mark Twain</u>

76. "My brethren, we can no more think about anything without a mental image than we can live without breathing. By the law of association, the material image calls up the mental idea and vice versa. This is why the Hindu uses an external symbol when he worships. He will tell you, it helps to keep his mind fixed on the Being to whom he prays." - <u>Swami Vivekanand on idol worship in</u>

<u>the Parliament of Religions, Chicago 19th Sept 1893</u>

77. "It is very easy to believe that the Hindus, who have been declining for seven hundred years, were highly civilized in the past. We cannot prove that it is not so. You know how many sciences had their origin in India. Mathematics began there. You are even today counting 1,2,3, etc. to zero, after Sanskrit figures, and you all know that algebra also originated in India, and that gravitation was known to the Indians thousands of years before Newton was born." - <u>Swami Vivekanand in a lecture delivered in Las Angeles on Jan 8, 1900</u>

78. "There are people in the world so hungry, that God cannot appear to them except in the form of bread." - <u>Gandhi</u>

79.  "Don't be too proud, don't be too arrogant; or else Nature will find a way to make you humble." - <u>Unknown</u>

80.  "The Eternal Religion, the religion of the rishis, has been in existence from time out of mind and will exist eternally. There exists in this *Sanatana Dharma* all forms of worship - worship of God with form and worship of the Impersonal Deity as well. It contains all paths - the path of knowledge, the path of devotion, and so on. Other forms of religion, the modern cults, will remain for a few days and then disappear." - <u>Sri Ramakrishna (Hinduism is also known as Eternal Religion or Sanatana Dharma)</u>

81.  "If you want to make an apple pie from scratch, you must first create the universe." - <u>Carl Sagan (1934-1996)</u>

82.  "After a study of some forty years and more of the great religions of the

world, I find none so perfect, none so scientific, none so philosophical, and none so spiritual than the great religion known by the name of Hinduism. Make no mistake, without Hinduism, India has no future. Hinduism is the soil into which India's roots are stuck and torn out of that she will inevitably wither as a tree torn out from its place. And if Hindus do not maintain Hinduism who shall save it? If India's own children do not cling to her faith who shall guard it. India alone can save India, and India and Hinduism are one." - Dr. Annie Besant (1847-1933)

83. "Thunder is good, thunder is impressive; but it is lightning that does the work." - Mark Twain

84. "Force your demands on God. He is by no means a stranger to you. He is

indeed your very own." - <u>Sri Ramakrishna</u>

85.  "Equality in all beings is the sign of the free." - <u>An ancient Sanskrit couplet</u>

86.  "It is good to repeat the name of Rama. The same Rama who was the son of King Dasaratha has created this world. Again, as Spirit, He pervades all beings. He is very near us; He is both within and without." - <u>Sri Ramakrishna</u>

87.  "When I read the Bhagavad-Gita and reflect about how God created this universe, everything else seems so superfluous." - <u>Albert Einstein</u>

88.  "Every time you point a finger in scorn - there are three remaining fingers pointing right back at you." - <u>Native American saying</u>

89.  "In the morning I bathe my intellect in the stupendous and cosmogonal

philosophy of the Bhagavad-Gita, in comparison with which our modern world and its literature seem puny and trivial." - <u>Henry David Thoreau</u>

90.  "The people of India, even the 'ignorant masses,' are by centuries of training nearer to the inner realities, than even the cultured elite anywhere else." - <u>Sri Aurobindo</u>

91.  "The Gita is the greatest gospel of spiritual works ever yet given to the race." - <u>Sri Aurobindo</u>

92.  "Surely, I can assure you of that a hundred times. But the prayer must be genuine and earnest. Do the worldly-minded people weep for God as they do for wife and children?" - <u>Sri Ramakrishna in response to the question *Does God listen to our prayers for Bhakti?*</u>

93.  "Truthfulness is the *tapasya* of *Kaliyuga*. Truthfulness, submission to God, and looking at the wives of other men as one's own mother - these are the means to realize God." - <u>Sri Ramakrishna</u>

94.  "We owe a lot to the Indians who taught us how to count, without which, no worthwhile scientific discovery could have been made." - <u>Albert Einstein</u>

95.  "I go into Upanishads to ask questions." - <u>Niels Bohr (1885-1962)</u>

96.  "The Indian way of life provides the vision of the natural, real way of life. We veil ourselves with unnatural masks. On the face of India are the tender expressions which carry the mark of the Creators hand." - <u>George Bernard Shaw (1856-1950)</u>

97. "This is the India of which I speak -
the India which, as I said, is to me the
Holy Land. For those who, though
born for this life in a Western land and
clad in a Western body, can yet look
back to earlier incarnations in which
they drank the milk of spiritual
wisdom from the breast of their true
mother - they must feel ever the
magic of her immemorial past, must
dwell ever under the spell of her
deathless fascination; for they are
bound to India by all the sacred
memories of their past; and with her,
too, are bound up all the radiant
hopes of their future, a future which
they know they will share with her
who is their true mother in the soul-
life." - <u>Dr. Annie Besant</u>

98. "Whenever I have read any part of the
Vedas, I have felt that some unearthly
and unknown light illuminated me. In
the great teaching of the Vedas, there

is no touch of sectarianism. It is of all ages, climes and nationalities and is the royal road for the attainment of the Great Knowledge. When I am at it, I feel that I am under the spangled heavens of a summer night." - <u>Henry David Thoreau</u>

99. "One sentence of the Bhagavad-Gita, is worth the State of Massachusetts many times over." - <u>Henry David Thoreau</u>

100. "I owed a magnificent day to the Bhagavad-Gita. It was as if an empire spoke to us, nothing small or unworthy, but large, serene, consistent, the voice of an old intelligence which in another age and climate had pondered and thus disposed of the same questions which exercise us." - <u>Ralph Waldo Emerson (1803-1882)</u>

101. "India - the one land that all men desire to see, and having once seen, by even a glimpse, would not give that glimpse for all the shows of all the rest of the globe combined." - Mark Twain

102. "It is very important to note that some 2,500 years ago at the least, Pythagoras went from Samos to the Ganga (Ganges) to learn geometry... But he would certainly not have undertaken such a strange journey had the reputation of the Brahmins' science not been long established in Europe..." - Voltaire

103. "If there is one place on the face of the earth where all the dreams of living men have found a home from the very earliest days when man began the dream of existence, it is India....For more than 30 centuries, the tree of vision, with all its thousand

branches and their millions of twigs, has sprung from this torrid land, the burning womb of the Gods. It renews itself tirelessly showing no signs of decay." - <u>Romaine Rolland (1866-1944)</u>

104. "God is realized by following the path of truth. One should always chant His name. Even while one is performing his duties, the mind should be left with God." - <u>Sri Ramakrishna</u>

105. "We are all calling on the same God. Jealousy and malice need not be. Some say that God is formless, and some that God has form. I say, let one man meditate on God with form if he believes in form, and let another meditate on the formless Deity if he does not believe in form. What I mean is that dogmatism is not good. It is not good to feel that my religion alone is true and other religions are

false. The correct attitude is this: My religion is right, but I do not know whether other religions are right or wrong, true or false. I say this because one cannot know the true nature of God unless one realizes Him." - <u>Sri Ramakrishna</u>

106. "God with form is my Mother, the formless is my Father. Which shall I blame? Which shall I praise? The pans of the scales are equally heavy." - <u>Kabir</u>

107. "God has been described in the Vedas as both with attributes and without. You describe Him as without form only. That is one-sided. But never mind. If you know one of His aspects truly, you will be able to know His other aspects too. God Himself will tell you all about them." - <u>Sri Ramakrishna pointing to some</u>

108. "Don't torment the poor, weak and helpless. Nobody - not even God Himself - can save you from the cry of their souls." - Tulsi and also Kabir

109. "Those who bear children of blameless character will be untouched by evil for seven births." - Tirukural 62

110. "The son's duty to his father is to make the world ask, 'By what great austerities did he merit such a son?'" - Tirukural 70

111. "Revealing an action after its completion is resoluteness. Disclosing an action midway causes endless misery." - Tirukural 663

112. "All the powers in the universe are already ours. It is we who have covered our eyes with both hands and

cry that it is dark." - <u>Swami Vivekanand</u>

113. "Of all virtues summed by ancient sages, the foremost is to share one's food and to protect all living creatures." - <u>Tirukural 322</u>

114. "By knowing his thoughts, a man's mind is discovered. By knowing his associates, his character is revealed." - <u>Tirukural 453</u>

115. "A sapling should be fenced all around to protect it from goats and cattle. When it grows and becomes a tree, the very animals who tried to destroy it, take shelter under it." - <u>Sri Ramakrishna on raising children</u>

116. "We are all equally poor...We are all striving for that extra buck." - <u>Unknown</u>

117. "Thinking is the hardest work there is, which is probably the reason why so few engage in it." - <u>Henry Ford (1863-1947)</u>

118. "I like to hire lazy people; they always come up with easier ways to do the things." - <u>Henry Ford</u>

119. "The problem with self-made people is that they worship their creator." - <u>Unknown</u>

120. "If you remain calm when others try to hurt you, then you are God." – <u>Swami Yoganand (1893-1952)</u>

121. "Love and charity for the whole human race; that is the test of true religiousness." - <u>Swami Vivekanand</u>

122. "The moment you seek Him, He will save you." - <u>Swami Vivekanand</u>

123. "God alone will never disappoint you." - <u>Swami Yoganand</u>

124. "Read only those books which have been written by persons who have had realization." - <u>Swami Vivekanand</u>

125. "I am amazed to see how much satisfaction a human being derives from humiliating a fellow human being." - <u>Gandhi</u>

126. "Our cells are constantly eavesdropping on our thoughts and being changed by them." - <u>Deepak Chopra</u>

127. "The first sign that you are becoming religious is that you are becoming cheerful." - <u>Swami Vivekanand</u>

128. "The only sure thing about luck is that it will change." - <u>Unknown</u>

129. "The further a society drifts from the truth, the more it will hate those that speak it." - George Orwell <u>(1903-1950)</u>

130. "If you're not invited to the wedding, don't attend the funeral." - <u>An adage on Wall Street</u>

131. "The value of a human being is determined not by his valuable possessions, but what he has given to others." - <u>Unknown</u>

132. "Life's most persistent and urgent question is, 'what are you doing for others?'" - <u>Martin Luther King, Jr. (1929-1968)</u>

133. "There are two signs of knowledge: first, absence of pride; and second, a peaceful nature." - <u>Unknown</u>

134. "Signs of inner sickness: (1) suspicion, (2) ill-will, (3) fear, and (4) greed." - <u>Sri Yukteshwar (1855-1936)</u>

135. "Five things to live by: (1) self-respect, (2) calmness, (3) determination, (4) simple diet, and (5) regular exercise." - <u>Sri Yukteshwar</u>

136. "You are only as good as your last act." - <u>An American proverb</u>

137. "If you can somehow keep your mind on God, all obstacles will go away. There is tremendous power in the name of God. Sing His name and glories." - <u>Sri Ramakrishna</u>

138. "He who rests in Me and gives up all other self-assertion and struggles, I carry to him whatever he needs." - <u>Shri Krishna in Bhagavad-Gita</u>

139. "I will become a Christian when I meet one." - <u>Gandhi to missionaries who tried to convert him to Christianity</u>

140. "Even if you kill me, my love for India will remain. My dead body will still be spreading the fragrance of that love." - <u>Shaheed Bhagat Singh (1907-1931), who burst into singing these words before his hanging by the British</u>

141. "An old error is always more popular than a new truth." - <u>German proverb</u>

142. "The more we study the brain, the more we unveil only glimpses of its true complexity." - <u>Russell Blaylock, MD, and Brain Surgeon in the USA,</u>

143. "I don't want to be in a profession where socializing outside the workplace is an important way to further your career." - <u>Unknown</u>

144. "It is not that I am so smart, it is just that I stay with the problems longer." - <u>Albert Einstein</u>

145. "What could be mightier than destiny? For it is present even in the plans we devise to overcome it." - <u>Tirukural 380</u>

146. "He degenerates who takes up the road to enjoyment...This truth never shines in the heart of those who are like ignorant children, deluded by a few lumps of earth." - <u>Swami Vivekanand</u>

147. "When someone starts hating you, remember that you are just so awesome!" - <u>Unknown</u>

148. "Once a society becomes successful it becomes arrogant, righteous, overconfident, corrupt and decadent...overspends...costly wars...wealth inequity and social tensions increase; and society enters a secular decline." - <u>Scottish Historian Alexander Tytler</u>

149. "In a democracy, people get the government they deserve." - <u>Alexis de Toqueville</u>

150. "All democracies commit suicide." - <u>John Adams (1735-1826), 2nd president of the United States</u>

151. "Sure, real estate, stocks, bonds and commodities are investments, but so are education, art, spirituality, vacations, health and children." - <u>Unknown</u>

152. "Intelligence never comes by attending the most prestigious schools and academies - it is in-built." - <u>Unknown</u>

153. "It is better to be a king of hell than a slave of heaven." - <u>Unknown</u>

154. "Anybody who tells you that he understands the American economy ought to be sent to teach modern

dance." - <u>Peter Drucker, Management Guru</u>

155. "I am the result of all my past." - <u>Swami Vivekanand</u>

156. "Your actions speak so loudly that I cannot hear what you say." - <u>Emerson</u>

157. "I do not believe in free will. Human beings in their thinking, feeling and acting are not free but are as casually bound as the stars in their motions. Jewish as well as Christian theologians believe in free will. They believe that man shapes his own life. I reject that doctrine. In that respect I am not a Jew." - <u>Albert Einstein</u>

158. "We are in the position of a little child entering a huge library filled with books in many languages. The child knows someone must have written those books. It does not know how. It does not understand the languages in

which they are written. The child dimly suspects a mysterious order in the arrangement of the books but doesn't know what it is. That, it seems to me, is the attitude of even the most intelligent human being toward God. We see the universe marvelously arranged and obeying certain laws but only dimly understand these laws. The problem involved is too vast for our limited minds." - <u>Albert Einstein</u>

159. "Try and penetrate with our limited means the secrets of nature and you will find that, behind all the discernible laws and connections, there remains something subtle, intangible and inexplicable. Veneration for this force beyond anything that we can comprehend is my religion. To that extent I am, in fact, religious." - <u>Albert Einstein</u>

160. "What separates me from most so-called atheists is a feeling of utter humility toward the unattainable secrets of the harmony of the cosmos." - <u>Albert Einstein</u>

161. "In corporate America, a pat on the back is only few inches away from a kick in the butt." - <u>Wall Street Adage</u>

162. "If a man does not know to what port he is sailing, no wind is favorable." - <u>Seneca</u>

163. "The present is theirs; the future, for which I really worked, is mine." - <u>Nikola Tesla (1856-1943)</u>

164. "When you help a poor man, do not feel the least pride. That is worship for you, and not the cause of pride." - <u>Swami Vivekanand</u>

165. "The world's great spiritual giants have all been produced only by those

religious sects which have been in possession of very rich mythology and ritual. All sects that have attempted to worship God without any form or ceremony have crushed without mercy everything that is beautiful and sublime in religion. Their religion is a fanaticism at best, a dry thing. The history of the world is a standing witness to this fact. Therefore do not decry these rituals and mythologies." - <u>Swami Vivekanand on The Ideal of a Universal Religion</u>

166. "It is better to be an outspoken atheist than a hypocrite." - <u>Swami Vivekanand</u>

167. "Silly fools tell you that you are sinners, and you sit down in a corner and weep. It is foolishness, wickedness, downright rascality to say that you are sinners!" - <u>Swami Vivekanand, to an American audience</u>

168. "If one does not take the standard of
reason, there cannot be any true
judgment. For instance, the
Mohammedan religion allows
Mohammedans to kill all who are not
of their religion. It is clearly stated in
the Koran, 'Kill the infidels if they do
not become Mohammedans.'  They
must be put to fire and sword. Now if
we tell a Mohammedan that this is
wrong, he will naturally ask, 'How do
you know that? How do you know it is
not good? My book says it is.' " -
Swami Vivekanand in London, 1896

169. "It is easy to hate and difficult to love.
This is how the whole scheme of
things works. All good things are
difficult to achieve, and bad things are

very easy to get." - <u>Confucius (551-479 BCE)</u>

170. "Without feelings of respect, what is there to distinguish men from beasts?" - <u>Confucius</u>

171. "Health is the greatest gift, contentment the greatest wealth, faithfulness the best relationship." - <u>Buddha (5th to 4th Century BCE)</u>

172. "A leader is a dealer in hope." - <u>Napoleon Bonaparte (1769-1821)</u>

173. "For general oral hygiene and disease-free gums, massage the gums with a mixture containing finely ground five parts [potassium] alum powder, two parts rock salt powder, three parts black pepper powder, and one part turmeric root powder." - <u>Ayurvedic medicinal guidance</u>

174. "For tooth pain and deep pocketed/loose gums, massage the gums with a mixture of licorice (मुलेठी) root powder, liquid Vitamin E (or wheat germ oil) and turmeric root powder (in equal amounts), at least twice a day." - <u>Ayurvedic medicinal guidance</u>

175. "Four traits define the true gentleman: a smiling face, a generous hand, a courteous demeanor, and kind words." - <u>Tirukural 953</u>

176. "Thank you!" - <u>Sri Ramakrishna's response in English when one of his disciples stated that "*The desire to argue disappears when a man attains wisdom.*"</u>

177. "Without hard work nothing can be achieved." - <u>An ancient Sanskrit proverb</u>

178. "It is God alone who has planted in man's mind what the 'Englishman' calls free will. People who have not realized God would become engaged in more and more sinful actions if God had not planted in them the notion of free will. Sin would have increased if God had not made the sinner feel that he alone was responsible for his sin." - <u>Sri Ramakrishna</u>

179. "Those who have realized God are aware that free will is a mere appearance. In reality man is the machine and God its Operator, man is the carriage and God its Driver." - <u>Sri Ramakrishna</u>

180. "A man is as free as a cow tethered to a tree" - <u>Sri Ramakrishna, quoting one of his devotees</u>

181. "God is born as man for the purpose of sporting as man. Rama, Krishna, and Chaitanya are examples. By

meditating on an Incarnation of God one meditates on God Himself." - <u>Sri Ramakrishna</u>

182. "What has the future in store for this strange being [man], born of breath, of perishable tissue, yet mortal, with his powers fearful and divine? What magic will be wrought by him in the end? What is to be his greatest deed, his crowning achievement? Long ago he recognized that all perceptible matter comes from a primary substance, or a tenuity beyond conception, filling all space, the *akasha* or luminiferous ether, which is acted upon by the life-giving *prana* or creative force, calling into existence, in never ending cycles, all things and phenomena. Can Man control this grandest, most awe-inspiring of all processes in nature? To do so would place him beside his Creator, make him fulfill his ultimate destiny." -

<u>Nikola Tesla, one of the greatest scientists ever born and inventor of AC electricity and the transformer (among many other things), who befriended Swami Vivekanand and was inspired by the Hindu view of the universe.</u>

183. "A man is never more truthful than when he acknowledges himself a liar." - <u>Mark Twain</u>

184. "Anger is an acid that can do more harm to the vessel in which it is stored than to anything on which it is poured." - <u>Mark Twain</u>

185. "Cauliflower is nothing but cabbage with a college education." - <u>Mark Twain</u>

186. "Everything has its limit - iron ore cannot be educated into gold." - <u>Mark Twain</u>

187. "Forgiveness is the fragrance that the violet sheds on the heel that has crushed it." - <u>Mark Twain</u>

188. "God made the Idiot for practice, and then He made the School Board." - <u>Mark Twain on pre-college education in America</u>

189. "If it's your job to eat a frog, it's best to do it first thing in the morning. And if it's your job to eat two frogs, it's best to eat the biggest one first." - <u>Mark Twain</u>

190. "The secret source of humor is not joy but sorrow; there is no humor in Heaven." - <u>Mark Twain</u>

191. "The right word may be effective, but no word was ever as effective as a rightly timed pause." - <u>Mark Twain</u>

192. "We have the best government that money can buy." - <u>Mark Twain, on the USA</u>

193. "Why is it that we rejoice at a birth and grieve at a funeral? It is because we are not the person involved." - <u>Mark Twain</u>

194. "Whatever you see and whatever you hear, will sooner or later have an effect on what you think and do." - <u>Morari Bapu</u>

195. "Access to the Vedas is the greatest privilege this century may claim over all previous centuries." - <u>J. Robert Oppenheimer (1904-1967), Father of the US Atomic Bomb</u>

196. "He who controls the past controls the future. He who controls the present controls the past." - <u>George Orwell</u>

197. "Christianity neither is, nor ever was, a part of the Common Law." - <u>Thomas Jefferson</u>

198. "Man as an individual is a genius. But men in the mass form the headless monster, a great brutish idiot that goes where prodded." - <u>Charlie Chaplin</u>

199. "He who has renounced the pleasure of a wife has verily renounced the pleasure of the world. God is very near to such a person." - <u>Sri Ramakrishna</u>

200. "You cannot get rid of ego until you have realized God. If you find a person free from ego, then know for certain that he has seen God." - <u>Sri Ramakrishna</u>

201. "Pray to God. He is full of compassion. Will He not listen to the words of His devotee? He is the

*Kalpataru.* You will get whatever you desire from Him." - <u>Sri Ramakrishna</u>

202. "The average age (longevity) of a meat eater is 63. I am on the verge of 85 and still work as hard as ever. I have lived quite long enough and am trying to die; but I simply cannot do it. A single beef-steak would finish me; but I cannot bring myself to swallow it. I am oppressed with a dread of living forever. That is the only disadvantage of vegetarianism." - <u>George Bernard Shaw</u>

203. "If slaughterhouses had glass walls, everyone would be a vegetarian." - <u>Paul McCartney</u>

204. "Cattle dragged and choked... knocking 'em four, five, ten times. They feel the approaching death. They do not want to die. Every now and then when they're stunned they come back to life, and they're up there

agonizing. They're supposed to be re-stunned but sometimes they aren't, and they'll go through the skinning process alive." - <u>A veteran USDA meat inspector from Texas describing what he saw, 'Slaughterhouse' (1997)</u>

205. "My situation is a solemn one. Life is offered to me on condition of eating beefsteaks. But death is better than cannibalism. My will contains directions for my funeral, which will be followed not by mourning coaches, but by oxen, sheep, flocks of poultry, and a small traveling aquarium of live fish, all wearing white scarfs in honor of the man who perished rather than eat his fellow creatures." - <u>George Bernard Shaw</u>

206. "I just could not stand the idea of eating meat - I really do think that it has made me calmer.... People's general awareness is getting much

better, even down to buying a pint of milk:  the fact that the calves are actually killed so that the milk doesn't go to them but to us cannot really be right, and if you have seen a cow in a state of extreme distress because it cannot understand why its calf isn't by, it can make you think a lot." - <u>Kate Bush, famous English singer-songwriter, musician, and record producer</u>

207. "Nothing will benefit human health and increase chances for survival of life on Earth as much as the evolution to a vegetarian diet." - <u>Albert Einstein</u>

208. "When the bad times come, they always let go of the smart people first. They can then easily hide their incompetence." - <u>Unknown, referring to Corporate America</u>

209. "We are indeed much more than what we eat, but what we eat can

nevertheless help us to be much more than what we are." - <u>Adelle Davis (1904 - 1974)</u>

210. "You cannot teach a man anything, you can only help him find it within himself." - <u>Galileo Galilei (1564-1642)</u>

211. "People who dismiss the unemployed and dependent as 'parasites' fail to understand economics and parasitism. A successful parasite is one that is not recognized by its host, one that can make its host work for it without appearing as a burden. Such is the ruling class in a capitalist society." - <u>Prof. Jason Read</u>

212. "When injustice becomes law, resistance becomes duty." - <u>Thomas Jefferson</u>

213. "If you don't have time to do it right, when will you have time to do it over?" - <u>John Wooden</u>

214. "If I had six hours to chop down a tree, I'd spent the first four sharpening the axe." - <u>Abraham Lincoln (1809-1865)</u>

215. "Words have the power to both destroy and heal. When words are both true and kind, they can change our world." - <u>Buddha</u>

216. "The price of apathy towards public affairs is to be ruled by evil men." - <u>Plato</u>

217. "Biology is really chemistry, chemistry is really physics, physics is really math, and math is really hard." - <u>Unknown</u>

218. "No matter how far down the wrong road you've gone, turn back." - <u>Turkish proverb</u>

219. "Wisdom is rooted in watching with affection the way people grow." - <u>Confucius</u>

220. "The reasonable man adapts himself to the world; the unreasonable persists in trying to adapt the world to himself. Therefore, all progress depends on the unreasonable man." - George Bernard Shaw

221. "In the sky, there is no distinction of east and west; people create distinctions out of their own minds and then believe them to be true." - Buddha

222. "Those who make peaceful revolution impossible will make violent revolution inevitable." - John F. Kennedy (1917-1963)

223. "Success does not consist in never making mistakes but in never making the same one a second time." - George Bernard Shaw

224. "Water, taken in moderation, cannot hurt anybody." - Mark Twain

225. "A banker is a fellow who lends you his umbrella when the sun is shining, but wants it back the minute it begins to rain." - <u>Mark Twain</u>

226. "An open mind has but one disadvantage: it collects dirt." - <u>Voltaire</u>

227. "We learn from history that we learn nothing from history." - <u>George Bernard Shaw</u>

228. "The opposite of a correct statement is a false statement. But the opposite of a profound truth may well be another profound truth." - <u>Niels Bohr</u>

229. "I know not with what weapons World War III will be fought, but World War IV will be fought with sticks and stones." - <u>Albert Einstein</u>

230. "I do not know what I may appear to the world, but to myself I seem to

have been only like a boy playing on the seashore, and diverting myself in now and then finding a smoother pebble or a prettier shell than ordinary, whilst the great ocean of truth lay all undiscovered before me."
- Sir Isaac Newton (1643-1727)

231. "Somewhere, something incredible is waiting to be known." - Carl Sagan

232. "Having the fewest wants, I am nearest to the gods." - Socrates (470-399 BCE)

233. "He who knows, does not speak. He who speaks, does not know." - Lao Tsu (4th Century BCE)

234. "Honesty is for the most part less profitable than dishonesty." - Plato

235. "God comes to you in the blind, in the halt, in the poor, in the weak, in the diabolical. What a glorious chance

for you to worship! The moment you think you are 'helping', you undo the whole thing and degrade yourself...It is blasphemy to think that you can help anyone" - <u>Swami Vivekanand in California, April 1, 1900</u>

236. "Work! Be unattached! That is the whole secret. If you get attached, you become miserable...Attach yourself to the Lord and to nothing else, because everything else is unreal. Attachment to the unreal will bring misery." - <u>Swami Vivekanand in California, April 1, 1900</u>

237. "Leaves and water and one flower - whosoever lays anything on my altar, I receive it with equal delight." - <u>Lord Krishna in Gita</u>

238. "The more selfish a man, the more immoral he is. And so also with race. That race which is bound down to itself has been the cruelest and the

most wicked in the whole world. There has not been a religion that has clung to this dualism more than that found by the prophet of Arabia, and there has not been a religion which has shed so much blood and been so cruel to other man. In the Koran there is the doctrine that a man who does not believe those teachings should be killed; it is considered a mercy to kill him! And the surest way to get to heaven, where there are beautiful houris and all sorts of self-enjoyments, is by killing these unbelievers. Think of the bloodshed there has been as a result of such beliefs!" - <u>Swami Vivekanand, London, 1896</u>

239. "As soon as you make a sect you protest against equality, and equality is no more. Mohammedans talk of universal brotherhood, but what comes out of that in reality? Why, anybody who is not a Mohammedan

will not be admitted into the brotherhood; he will more likely have his throat cut. Christians talk of universal brotherhood; but anyone who is not a Christian must go to that place where he will be eternally barbecued...So those who really feel at heart the universal brotherhood of man, do not talk much, do not make little sects for universal brotherhood...This world is too full of blustering talk." - <u>Swami Vivekanand on The Ideal of a Universal Religion</u>

240. "One who knows Aum knows God." - <u>Patanjali (~3000 BCE), a great Sage of ancient India and the author of Yoga Sutra</u>

241. "If one has always spoken the truth, whatever he utters from his mouth shall come to pass." - <u>Sage Patanjali. Swami Vivekanand affirmed this statement. Upon asking "how long</u>

one has to practice this austerity of truthfulness before one begets such powers", Swamiji answered "twelve years."

242. "Varanasi or Banaras is older than history, older than tradition, older even than legend, and looks twice as old as all of them put together." - Mark Twain

243. "India has two million gods, and worships them all. In religion all other countries are paupers; India is the only millionaire." - Mark Twain

244. "India had the start of the whole world in the beginning of things. She had the first civilization; she had the first accumulation of material wealth; she was populous with deep thinkers and subtle intellect; she had mines, and woods, and a fruitful soul." - Mark Twain

245. "India was a victim of the mischief wrought by Christian missionaries." - <u>Dr. Annie Besant</u>

246. "The year 1863 will remain dear and blessed to me. 'Why? Because I had read India's sacred poem, the Ramayana - Divine poem, ocean of milk!' " - <u>French historian Jules Michelet (1798-1874)</u>

247. "India was the motherland of our race, and Sanskrit the mother of Europe's languages: she was the mother of our philosophy; mother, through the Arabs, of much of our mathematics; mother, through the Buddha, of the ideals embodied in Christianity; mother, through the village community, of self-government and democracy. Mother India is in many ways the mother of us all." - <u>Will Durant (1885-1981), American Historian</u>

248. "Hinduism, Buddhism and Taoism stating clearly that History centric religions indeed are driven by conquest mentality and hence potential for violence exists all the time because of the 'Market share' and conversion mentality." - <u>Aldous Huxley (1894-1963), English novelist</u>

249. "The religions whose theology is least preoccupied with events in time and most concerned with eternity, have been consistently less violent and more humane in political practice. Unlike early Judaism, Christianity, and Mohammedanism (all obsessed with time), Hinduism and Buddhism have never been persecuting faiths, have preached almost no holy wars and have refrained from that proselytizing religious imperialism which has gone hand in hand with political and economic oppression of colored people." - <u>Aldous Huxley</u>

250. "Vedanta is the most impressive metaphysics the human mind has conceived." - <u>Alfred North Whitehead (1861-1947), British mathematician, logician, and philosopher</u>

251. "We must respect the other fellow's religion, but only in the sense and to the extent that we respect his theory that his wife is beautiful and his children smart." - <u>Henry Louis Mencken (1880-1956), also known as Sage of Baltimore</u>

252. "Democracy is also a form of worship. It is the worship of jackals by jackasses." - <u>Henry Louis Mencken</u>

253. "A man may be a fool and not know it - but not if he is married." - <u>Henry Louis Mencken</u>

254. "The trouble with Communism is the Communists, just as the trouble with

Christianity is the Christians." - <u>Henry Louis Mencken</u>

255. "Those who can, do. Those who can't, teach." - <u>George Bernard Shaw (in slightly different wordings)</u>

256. "Those desiring greatness must desire modesty. Those seeking their family's honor must seek to be respectful to all." - <u>Tirukural 960</u>

257. "What good is a body perfect in outer ways, if inwardly it is impaired by a lack of love?" - <u>Tirukural 79</u>

258. "Power tends to corrupt and absolute power corrupts absolutely. Great men are almost always bad men." - <u>Lord Acton, historian and moralist</u>

259. "If someone wants to understand India, he should read Vivekanand." - <u>Ravindranath Tagore (1861-1941)</u>

260. "Being the richest man in the cemetery doesn't matter to me. ...Going to bed at night saying we've done something wonderful - that's what matters to me." - <u>Steve Jobs (1955-2011)</u>

261. "If you lose wealth, you have lost nothing. If you lose health, you have lost something. If you lose character, you have lost everything." - <u>An Indian Proverb</u>

262. "I cannot give you the formula for success, but I can give you the formula for failure - which is: Try to please everybody." - <u>Herbert B. Swope (1882-1958), Greatest American journalist of his time</u>

263. "I have travelled across the length and breadth of India and I have not seen one person who is a beggar, who is a thief; such wealth I have seen in this country, such high moral values, people of such caliber, that I do not think we

would ever conquer this country unless we break the very backbone of this nation, which is her spiritual and cultural heritage and, therefore, I propose that we replace her old and ancient education system, her culture; for if the Indians think that all that is foreign and English is good and greater than their own, they will lose their self-esteem, the native culture, and they will become what we want them, a truly dominated nation." - Thomas Babington Macaulay in his address to the British Parliament in 1835

264. "An equation for me has no meaning, unless it expresses a thought of God." - Srinivasa Ramanujan (1887-1920), a math genius who was the second youngest inductee (at age 31) into the Royal Society, historically the most renowned world body of science. The only younger inductee was Sir Isaac Newton (at age 29)

265. "In battle, in the forest, at the precipice in the mountains, on the dark great sea, in the midst of javelins and arrows, in sleep, in confusion, in the depths of shame, the good deeds a man has done before defend him." - From Bhagavad-Gita; this verse was used by J. Oppenheimer in the final days of the Manhattan project

266. "I hate Indians. They are a beastly people with a beastly religion." - Winston Churchill, the racist and snobbish Prime Minister of UK during World War II

267. "The American sense of equality and human dignity is mainly limited to men of white skins. Even among these, there are prejudices of which I as a Jew am clearly conscious, but they are unimportant in comparison with the attitude of the 'Whites' toward their fellow-citizens of darker complexion, particularly toward Negroes. The more I

feel an American, the more this situation pains me. I can escape the feeling of complicity in it only by speaking out." - <u>Albert Einstein in "Dead Sea Scrolls of Physics"</u>

268. "I am firmly convinced that whoever believes that blacks are not our equals in intelligence, sense of responsibility, and reliability suffers from a fatal misconception. Your ancestors dragged these black people from their homes by force; and in the white man's quest for wealth and an easy life they have been ruthlessly suppressed and exploited, degraded into slavery. The modern prejudice against Negroes is the result of the desire to maintain this unworthy condition." - <u>Albert Einstein in "Dead Sea Scrolls of Physics"</u>

269. "Nearly all man can stand adversity, but if you want to test a man's

character, give him power." - <u>Abraham Lincoln</u>

270. "Give power to someone who does not deserve it, and he will know how to abuse it." - <u>Unknown</u>

271. "You have to have a stomach to digest gold." - <u>Indian proverb</u>

272. "Math is food for the brain. Music is food for the soul." - <u>Unknown</u>

273. "Comparison is a thief of joy." - <u>Theodore Roosevelt (1858-1919)</u>

274. "The only place where success comes before work is in the dictionary." - <u>Vidal Sassoon (1928-2012)</u>

275. "Most of the important things in the world have been accomplished by people who have kept on trying when there seemed to be no help at all." - <u>Dale Carnegie (1888-1955)</u>

276. "India is the only country in the world where history written by foreign historians is taught in textbooks." - <u>Nobel laureate V.S. Naipaul (1932-2018), in his book 'India: A Wounded Civilization'</u>

277. "A people without the knowledge of their past history, origin, and culture is like a tree without roots." - <u>Marcus Garvey (1887-1940)</u>

278. "What we know is dwarfed by what we don't know. The only sensible response is to be humble." - <u>Unknown</u>

279. "People spend an hour on the internet and think they know physics." - <u>Noam Chomsky, Professor Emeritus at MIT, linguist, and author of more than 100 books</u>

280. "Discoveries and inventions arise from observations of little things." - <u>Alexander Bell (1847-1922)</u>

281. "If a man says he's not afraid of dying, he's either lying, or he's a Gorkha." - <u>Indian Field Marshal Manekshaw (1914-2008), a Hero of the 1971 Indo-Pakistan War</u>

282. "If death strikes, before I prove my blood, I swear I'll kill death." - <u>Capt. Manoj Kumar Pandey of Gorkha Rifles - Indian Army who was awarded the Param Veer Chakra, India's highest honor for bravery</u>

283. "I regret I have but one life to give for my country." - <u>Indian Army Officer Prem Ramchandani</u>

284. "I never let schooling interfere with my education." - <u>Mark Twain</u>

285. "Known is a drop, where unknown is an ocean." - <u>Unknown</u>

286. "To be successful you need friends and to be very successful you need

enemies." - <u>Novelist Sidney Sheldon, on American Foreign Policy</u>

287. "All generalizations are false, including this one." - <u>Mark Twain</u>

288. "Woman exists for man as long as he has lust. When you are free from lust, you don't see any difference between the sexes." - <u>Swami Vivekanand</u>

289. "He alone is worshipping God, who serves all beings." - <u>Swami Vivekanand</u>

290. "Caste is a state, not an iron-bound class." - <u>Swami Vivekanand</u>

291. "Being smart is good. But being disciplined is more valuable in the long run." - <u>Wall Street Adage</u>

292. "Those who do not remember the past are condemned to repeat it." - <u>George Santayana (1863-1952)</u>

293. "Natural processes within us are the true healers of disease." - <u>Hippocrates</u>

294. "Absence of evidence is not evidence of absence." - <u>Traditional catch phrase used by astrophysicist Dr. Carl Sagan to support presence of life somewhere in the universe</u>

295. "If you don't read the newspaper, you're uninformed. If you read the newspaper, you're misinformed." - <u>Mark Twain</u>

296. "When everything seems to be going against you, remember that the airplane takes off against the wind, not with it." - <u>Henry Ford</u>

297. "I am not a product of my circumstances. I am a product of my decisions." - <u>Stephen Covey</u>

298. "As I grow older, I pay less attention to what men say. I just watch what they do." - <u>Andrew Carnegie (1835-1919)</u>

299. "Cowards die many times before their deaths; the valiant never taste death but once." - <u>William Shakespeare (1564-1616)</u>

300. "Everyone sees what you appear to be; few really know what you are." - <u>Niccolo Machiavelli (1469-1527)</u>

301. "Few men are born brave; many become so through training and force of discipline." <u>Vegetius (late 4<sup>th</sup> Century)</u>

302. "Great empires are not maintained by timidity." - <u>Cornelius Tacitus (56-120 CE)</u>

303. "I do not think that there is any other quality so essential to success of any kind as the quality of perseverance. It overcomes almost everything, even

nature." - <u>John D. Rockefeller (1839-1937)</u>

304. "I don't want a nation of thinkers; I want a nation of workers." - <u>John D. Rockefeller</u>

305. "I emphasize that I am full of ambition and hope and of full charm of life. But I can renounce all at the time of need, and that is the real sacrifice." - <u>Bhagat Singh</u>

306. "I know of nothing more despicable and pathetic than a man who devotes all the hours of the waking day to the making of money for money's sake." - <u>John D. Rockefeller</u>

307. "If a man does not know to what port he is sailing, no wind is favorable." - <u>Seneca (Roman writer)</u>

308. "If an elderly but distinguished scientist says that something is possible

he is almost certainly right, but if he says that it is impossible he is very probably wrong." - <u>Arthur C. Clarke (1917-2008)</u>

309. "If the only tool you have is a hammer, you tend to see every problem as a nail." - <u>Abraham Maslow (1908-1970)</u>

310. "In any moment of decision, the best thing you can do is the right thing, the next best thing is the wrong thing, and the worst thing you can do is nothing." - <u>Theodore Roosevelt</u>

311. "Let them hate us as long as they fear us." - <u>Caligula (3rd Roman Emperor)</u>

312. "Our task must be to free ourselves from this prison by widening our circle of compassion to embrace all living creatures and the whole of nature in its beauty." - <u>Albert Einstein</u>

313. "The weak can never forgive.
Forgiveness is the attribute of the
strong." - Gandhi

314. "If you have fear, you must quit." -
Indian Field Marshal Manekshaw

315. "If you want to know what will happen
tomorrow, one thing that will happen to
you is you will not play today's game
well." - Sadhguru Vasudev, Indian yogi
and author

316. "Alms with kindness; knowledge with
humility; wealth with simplicity; and
strength with patience." - Adi
Sankaracharya, Indian philosopher and
theologian, on the four pillars of Hindu
living

317. "O my mothers and sisters of Bharat,
do not forget that your ideal is the ideal
of Seeta, Savitri and Dayamanti. Do not
forget that your Ishwar is purer than the
purest Umapati Shiva. For your marriage

is not only for wealth, and life is not
only for sense pleasure. Nor all this is
for your personal gain. You are born to
be sacrificed on the altar of Mother
Durga. Social norms and traditions are
nothing but for unending world of
motherhood." - Swami Vivekanand

318. "Dream is not what you see in sleep. It
is something which doesn't let you
sleep." - Eminent engineer and former
President of India APJ Kalam

319. "If you want God to laugh, tell Him
your plans." - American Proverb

320. "Man needs his difficulties because
they are necessary to enjoy success." -
APJ Kalam

321. "It is very easy to defeat someone. But
it is very hard to win someone." - APJ
Kalam

322. "Everything around you is your teacher." - <u>Unknown</u>

323. "Whatever others think or do, lower not your standard of Purity, Morality and Love of God." - <u>Swami Vivekanand</u>

324. "He who thinks himself weak, will become weak." - <u>Swami Vivekanand</u>

325. "Upon ages of struggle, a character is built." - <u>Swami Vivekanand</u>

326. "None but the dead have free speech." - <u>Mark Twain</u>

327. "This is a land, where anything that can ever be done either by man or God, has been done." - <u>Mark Twain after visiting India, the Himalayas, the yogis and mystics</u>

328. "The love which is in you, if it is given to any human being, will sooner or later bring pain and sorrow as the result. Our love must, therefore, be given to the

Highest One, to Him in the ocean of whose love there is neither ebb nor flow. Love must get to its right destination, it must go unto Him, the infinite ocean of love. All rivers flow into the ocean." - <u>Swami Vivekanand on loving everyone as *Atma* (soul) which is part of the same *Param-atma* (Super-Soul or God)</u>

329. "There seems to be some perverse human characteristic that likes to make easy things difficult." - <u>Warren Buffett</u>

330. "If you are feeling good, wait for a few moments; you will get over it." - <u>Unknown</u>

331. "A bad name is worse than a bad man." - <u>Indian Proverb</u>

332. "A smile is an inexpensive way to change your looks." - <u>Charles Gordy</u>

333. "Men, in general, judge more from appearance than from reality. All men have eyes, but few have the gift of penetration." - <u>Niccolo Machiavelli</u>

334. "Don't judge men's wealth or godliness by their Sunday appearance." - <u>Benjamin Franklin (1706-1790)</u>

335. "Your ego is directly proportional to the size of your house." - <u>Unknown</u>

336. "No one can take advantage of you without your permission." - <u>Dr. Laura Schlessinger, psychologist, and National Radio Hall of Fame member</u>

337. "Intuition does not come to unprepared minds." - <u>Unknown</u>

338. "How can a "free" press be owned?" - <u>Unknown</u>

339. "If a man is himself upside down, the whole world appears upside down to

him. A bad man always sees the whole world as bad." - <u>Unknown</u>

340. "Don't worry about the world coming to an end today. It is already tomorrow in Australia." - <u>Charles M. Schulz, influential American cartoonist</u>

341. "Positive thinkers have a solution for every problem. Negative thinkers have a problem with every solution." - <u>Unknown</u>

342. "I have not failed. I've just found 10,000 ways that won't work." - <u>Thomas Edison, a hugely productive inventor</u>

343. "The biggest truth is that anyone attempting to run away from death is actually running towards it...every passing moment pulls him closer and closer to death." - <u>Srimad Bhagavatam</u>

344. "Unthinking respect for authority is the greatest enemy of truth." - Albert Einstein

345. "Life is like riding a bicycle. To keep your balance you must keep moving." - Albert Einstein

346. "If I had the Gorkha, I could win the whole world." - Adolf Hitler

347. "No one wants to die. Even people who want to go to heaven don't want to die to get there. And yet death is the destination we all share." - Steve Jobs

348. "Those who wish to sing always find a song." - Swedish Proverb

349. "I began to sense that conventional science is inadequate for situations where the mind is involved. Ultimately, my work on the brain is more significant than my Nobel-prize winning research."

- <u>Brian D. Josephson, 1973 Nobel Prize winner in physics</u>

350. "India is the only major civilizational country where you are systematically taught to hate your heritage and glorify the invaders who came to destroy it. And this absurdity is called 'secularism'."
- <u>Tarek Fatah, Canadian rationalist, journalist and a Muslim, who is fighting for the freedom of Baluchistan from Pakistan</u>

351. "Nobody ever changed the world on 40 hours a week." - <u>Elon Musk, founder of electric car maker Tesla Inc., and SpaceX</u>

352. "I am Hindu, only because you are Muslim. Otherwise, I was a humanist." - <u>Veer Savarkar, the author of "The Indian War of Independence" and "Indian Rebellion of 1857" books banned by British authorities, was an Indian freedom activist who was imprisoned</u>

353. "Krishna of Purana, Shiva of Tantra, and Aum of Vedanta are all one and the same." - Sri Ramakrishna

354. "If you can't find one reason to be happy even in 'hell', you would surely find at least one reason to be unhappy in 'heaven.'" - Unknown

355. "One ounce of the practice of righteousness and of spiritual Self-realization outweighs tons and tons of frothy talk and nonsensical sentiments. Show us one, but one gigantic spiritual genius growing out of all this dry dust of ignorance and fanaticism; and if you cannot, close your mouths, open the windows of your hearts to the clear light of truth, and sit like children at the feet of those who know what they are talking about - the sages and saints. Let us then listen attentively to what they say." - Swami Vivekanand, delivered in New York, 1896

356. "India is, the cradle of human race, the birthplace of the human speech, the mother of history, the grandmother of legend, and the great grandmother of tradition. Our most valuable and most instructive materials in the history of man are treasured up in India only." - <u>Mark Twain</u>

357. "History is witness. A son who doesn't respect his parents can never be happy." - <u>Unknown</u>

358. "The doctrine that all men are equal, or have been at any time free and equal, is an utterly baseless fiction." - <u>Thomas Huxley (1825-1895), English biologist and anthropologist</u>

359. "Some people are educated beyond their intelligence." - <u>Jerry Clower, American stand-up comedian</u>

360. "Ask not what your country can do for you, ask what you can do for your country." - <u>John F. Kennedy, 35th president of the USA, in his inaugural</u>

address, considered among the best presidential inaugural speeches in American history

361. "Let us never negotiate out of fear. But let us never fear to negotiate." - John F. Kennedy

362. "Thoughts are contagious." - Swami Shivanand, Hindu spiritual scholar and a yogi

363. "Without God's grace, no amount of hard work will succeed." - Baba Neeb Karori (also known as Baba Neem Karoli), a God-like omnipotent, omniscient, and omnipresent saint in whose *Ashram* in India Steve Jobs and Mark Zuckerberg once lived

364. "Everyone is poor before God." - Baba Neeb Karori

365. "Whatever outer work you must do, do it; but train your mind in such a way that in your subconscious mind you are

always remembering God." - <u>Baba Neeb Karori</u>

366. "God listens to those who are happy with other's happiness and sad with their sadness. Jealousy is the biggest violence man can ever commit." - <u>Unknown</u>

367. "All that glitters is not gold." - <u>William Shakespeare</u>

368. "Don't talk too much, your ignorance exceeds your knowledge." - <u>Spanish proverb</u>

369. "Those who drown are the ones who know how to swim." - <u>Unknown</u>

370. "Find something you love to do, and you'll never have to work a day in your life." - <u>Princeton Alumni Weekly, 1982 (incorrectly credited to Confucius by his overzealous admirers)</u>

371. "If you want to be somebody in your life, learn to appreciate the accomplishment of others." - <u>Unknown</u>

372. "You can't be nice to bad people." - <u>Unknown</u>

373. "One who takes a cold shower has a strong will and a healthy body." - <u>Unknown</u>

374. "The only thing worse than starting something and failing...is not starting something." - <u>Seth Godin, American author and business executive</u>

375. "The spiritual aspiration is innate in man; for he is, unlike the animal, aware of imperfection and limitation and feels that there is something to be attained beyond what he now is." - <u>Sri Aurobindo</u>

376. "People who buy a daily latte are peeing $1 million down the drain as you

are drinking that coffee." - <u>T.C.U.
Orman, celebrity financial adviser</u>

377. "Artists and idiots are born, not made."
- <u>Charlie Chaplin</u>

378. "In any society, you are judged by the
company you keep and the people you
admire. On a professional level, you are
judged by the words you use." -
<u>Unknown</u>

379. "We are on a long journey, birth to
birth to birth. The people we meet in
each birth, we are predestined to meet."
- <u>Baba Neeb Karori</u>

380. "Only patriotism can infuse a sense of
selflessness in a man." - <u>Nambi
Narayanan, Author of *Ready to Fire*
(2018), a bright ISRO engineer, and a
key player in India's space program,
who was framed and incarcerated on
false charges of leaking India's space
secrets</u>

381. "I possess the key to all." - <u>Baba Neeb Karori</u>

382. "To sin by silence, when you should protest, makes cowards out of men." - <u>Ella Wheeler Wilcox, American author and poet</u>

383. "Reading is to the mind what exercise is to the body." - <u>Joseph Addison, English poet, playwrite and politician</u>

384. "The moment I stand in reverence before every human being and see God in him, that moment I am free." - <u>Swami Vivekanand as quoted by the U S president in his visit to India on February 24, 2020</u>

385. "Statistics are the basis for stereotyping." - <u>Unknown</u>

386. "Happiness is not the absence of problems, but the ability to deal with them." - <u>Buddha</u>

387. "Justice delayed is justice denied." - <u>A legal maxim in America</u>

388. "Great spirits have always encountered violent opposition from mediocre minds." - <u>Albert Einstein</u>

389. "Keep the name of Rama always in your mind, remembering it with love. It will feed you when you're alone, bless you when you're cursed, and protect you when you are abandoned. To the crippled it's another limb. To the blind it's another eye. To the orphaned it's a loving parent." - <u>Tulsi</u>

390. एकं सद्विप्रा बहुधा वदन्ति ।

That which exists is One; sages call It by various names. - <u>Vedas</u>

391. आलस्यं हि मनुष्याणां शरीरस्थो महारिपुः ।
नास्त्युद्यमसमो बन्धुः कृत्वा यं नावसीदति ॥

Laziness is verily a great enemy residing in our body. There is no friend

like hard work, doing which one does
not decline or become unhappy.

392. व्यायामात् लभते स्वास्थ्यम् , दीर्घायुषं बलं सुखं ।
आरोग्यं परमं भाग्यं, स्वास्थ्यम् सर्वार्थ साधनं ॥

Only with physical exercise does one
beget good health, long life, strength,
and happiness. The healthy body is a
great gift, and only because of good
health is all work possible.

393. रहिमन पानी राखिये, बिन पानी सब सून ।
पानी बिन ना ऊबरे, मोती मानुष चून ॥

[Poet Rahim uses three meanings of
*paani* in this couplet.] Rahim says paani
is worthy of possession; without paani
everything is void. Without paani
(meaning shine/luster or *aabha*), a
pearl does not have much value;
without paani (meaning humility, self-
respect or honor), a man lacks
worthiness; and with paani (meaning

water) only flour becomes soft and worthy of making bread.

394. जो रहीम उत्तम प्रकृति, का करि सकत कुसंग।
चंदन विष व्यापत नहीं, लपटे रहे भुजंग॥

What can bad company do to someone who has great innate nature? Snakes like to wrap themselves around the branches of a sandalwood tree, yet not affecting the very nature of the tree. - Rahim

395. नमंति फलिनो वृक्षाः, नमंति गुणिजनोः।
मूर्खाश्च, शुष्क वृक्षाश्चं, नमंति न कदाचन॥

When a tree is loaded with fruits, its branches bow down. A person of great qualities also bows down in humility. Dead trees and fools never bow down.

Purport: That which knows how to bend will not break.

396. तुलसी हाय गरीब की, कभी न निष्फल जाय।
मरी खाल की सॉस सो, लौह भस्म हो जाय॥

Never torment the poor, weak and helpless. The cry coming from the depths of their souls will never fail to destroy you. Even leather bellows made from the skin of poor dead cattle [in a blacksmith's workshop] can decimate steel. - <u>Tulsi</u>

397. तरूवर फल नहि खात है, सरवर पियत न पान ।
    कहि रहीम पर काज हित, संपति सचहिं सुजान ॥

A tree does not eat its own fruits, and a river does not drink its own water. They only work for others. Similarly, virtuous and pious people collect wealth for the good of others. - <u>Rahim</u>

398. दौलत में है दोलता, तुलसी निश्चय चीह्न ।
    आवे तो अंधा करे, जावे तो मतिहीन ॥

Know that *Doulata* (wealth) has *dou* (two) *lata* (identities or branches). When it (wealth) comes it makes you blind, and when it leaves it makes you mindless.

399. बिगड़ी बात बने नहीं, लाख करे किन कोय।
रहिमन बिगड़े दूध से, मथे न माखन होय॥

Once an idea (*baat*) is mismanaged
and derailed, it is very difficult to bring
it back on track, just like it is impossible
to make butter from the milk that has
gone bad. - <u>Rahim</u>

400. माखी गुड़ में गड़ी रहे, पंख रहे लपिटाय।
हाथ मले और सिर धुने, लालच बुरी बलाय॥

Greed gets you in trouble and is
extremely difficult to overcome. A
housefly attracted to molasses (greed)
cannot get out no matter how hard it
tries.

401. बड़ा हुआ तो क्या हुआ, जैसे पेड़ खजूर।
पंथी को छाया नहीं, फल लागे अति दूर॥

Being big in society means little. Don't
be like a date tree, which does not
provide shade to travelers, and the
fruits are too high up to reach.

402. बिना बिचारे जो करे, सो पीछे पछताय।

काम बिगारो आपना, जग मे होत हॅसाय ॥

A plan without thorough thinking will
only make you regretful. First, your
work will be ruined, and second,
people will laugh at you.

403. जो रहीम ओछो बढ़े, तो ही बा इतराय ।
     प्यादे से फर्जी भयो, टेढ़ो टेढ़ो जाय ॥

When an undeserving person gains
power, he develops an undesirable
attitude, just like a pawn in chess
begins to move differently (diagonally)
after getting promoted. - <u>Rahim</u>

404. क्षमा बड़न को चाहिये, छोटन को उतपात ।
     का रहीम हरि जो घट्यो, जो भृगु मारि लात ॥

It is befitting of good people to forgive
the faults of others. Even after being
kicked in the chest, the almighty *Hari*
conveniently forgave *Bhrigu*. - <u>Rahim</u>

405. तैं रहीम मन आपनो, कीन्हों चारू चकोर ।
     निसि वासर लाग्यो रहै, कृष्णचंद की ओर ॥

One who has made his mind pure and beautiful keeps looking unceasingly up to Lord Krishna, like the *Chakor* bird (compared here to a pure-minded person) loves to hypnotizingly look at the moon (compared here to Lord Krishna). - <u>Rahim</u>

406. एक साधे सब सधै, सब साधे सब जाय ।
रहिमन मूलहिं सांचिबो, फूलै फलै अघात ॥

If you are trying to achieve multiple goals through multiple means, they may all slip out of hand. Conversely, if you nourish One goal (referring to God), all goals will be accomplished. It is futile to water leaves, flowers, branches, fruits, stems, etc. You are better off watering the roots; you will get a beautiful tree with plenty of fruits. - <u>Rahim</u>

407. जो गरीब सों हित करे, धनि रहीम वे लोग ।
कहा सुदामा बापुरो, कृष्ण मिताई जोग ॥

Only those who help the poor are truly rich. Look how *Krishna*, the richest One, took care of utterly poor *Sudama*. - Rahim

408. जो बड़न को लघु कहे, नहि रहीम घट जात।
गिरिधर मुरलीधर कहे, कछु दुख मानत नाहि॥

Those who call great people by trivial names do not damage the value of the latter. People call Lord *Krishna* by names like bearer-of-the-hill or flute-bearer; still the Lord does not mind. - Rahim

409. रहिमन धागा प्रेम का, मत तोड़ो चिटकाय।
टूटे से फिर ना जुड़े, जुड़े गाँठ पड़ जाय॥

Do not snap the thread of love. Once broken, it cannot be rejoined. Even if the broken pieces are tied together, a knot forever remains. - Rahim

410. ऐसी बानी बोलिये, मन का आपा खोय।
औरन को शीतल करे, आपहु शीतल होय॥

Speaking humbly will soothe and calm others, in the process making yourself peaceful and serene.

411. साईं इतना दीजिये, जा में कुटुंब समाय ।
मैं भी भूखा ना रहूँ, साधू ना भूखा जाय ॥

O Lord, give me just enough so that I can take care of my family and not go hungry, and that no saint leaves my home without food. - <u>Kabir</u>

412. बुरा जो देखन मैं चला, बुरा न मिलया कोय ।
जो मन खोजा आपना, मुझसे बुरा न कोय ॥

I set out to look for a bad person, but couldn't find one. When I looked within, I *was* that bad person. - <u>Kabir</u>

413. राम नाम की लूट है, लूट सके तो लूट ।
पाछे फिर पछताये का, प्राण जाहिं जब छूट ॥

The name of *Rama* (powerful, consecrated *mantra* and a name of almighty God) is the greatest wealth, and is available for free. Take as much as possible before life comes to an end. - <u>Kabir</u>

414. जहॉ दया तहँ धर्म है, जहॉ लोभ तहँ पाप ।
      जहॉ क्रोध तहँ नाश है, जहॉ क्षमा वहँ आप ॥

Where there is compassion and kindness, there is *dharma* (religion); where there is greed, there is sin; where there is anger, there is self-destruction; where there is forgiveness, there is God.

415. शीलवंत सबसे बड़ा, सब रतन की खान ।
      तीन लोक की संपदा, रही शील की आन ॥

A person with *Sheel* (truthfulness, humility, compassion, forgiveness, calmness, good behavior, and character) is like a diamond mine. All the wealth in this world is useless without *sheel*.

416. निर्मल मन जन सो मोहि पावा ।
      मोहि कपट छल छिद्र न भावा ॥

Only those with a pure heart can find me. I do not like hypocrisy, deception, delusion, or treachery. - <u>Lord Rama, in Ramayan</u>

417. कस्तूरी कुंडल बसे, मृग ढूँढत बन माहि ।
ज्यो घट घट राम है, दुनिया देखे नाहि ॥

Musk from the musk-deer (fragrance from glandular secretions) exists within the deer itself, but the deer keeps searching for it throughout the forest. Similarly, *Rama* (God) is within us, but the world fails to recognize that. - <u>Kabir</u>

418. साधू शब्द समुंदर है, जा में रतन भराय ।
मंदभाग मुट्ठी भरे, कंकर हाथ लगाय ॥

The words of a saint are like an ocean full of treasure. However, those who are unfortunate [to stay away from saints] do not end up with more than a handful of pebbles.

419. दुख में सुमिरन सब करे, सुख में करे ना कोय ।

जो सुख में सुमिरन करे, तो दुख काहे होय ॥

Everybody remembers God in times of sorrow, but nobody does so when enjoying good times. But if they remember Him in good times, how can there be bad times?

420. सबसे लघुताई भली, लघुता से सब होय ।
जस दुतिया का चंद्रमा, शशिनवे सब कोय ॥

Considering oneself as *small* (e.g. modest, humble) is praiseworthy, that makes everything possible. Everyone admires the moon when it is the smallest. [The day after the new moon is considered holy in many Asian traditions.]

421. पत्ता टूटा डाल से, ले गयी पवन उड़ाय ।
अबके बिछुरे कबहु मिले, दूर पड़े है जाय ॥

[This couplet by Kabir is deeply metaphorical and talks about the separation of a dead leaf from a tree, symbolizing the separation of the human soul from the Creator.]

Worldly attractions (wind) have taken the soul (dead leaf) too far from the Divine (tree). When will these two meet again? When will the soul come back and merge with the creator and be released from the cycle of birth and death?

Another meaning could be: Once you are separated from your loved ones [at death], when will you meet again? Once a moment or situation has gone by, when will that be possible to bring it back?

422. जैसा भोजन खाईये, तैसा ही मन होय ।
　　 जैसा पानी पीजिये, तैसी बानी होय ॥

As is your food, so will be your mind. As is your *paani*, so will be your speech. (*Paani* here has two meanings: water and humility/Godliness.)

423. पतिव्रता मैली भली, काली कुचल कुरूप ।
　　 पतिव्रता के रूप पर, बारो कोटि सरूप ॥

A pious wife, despite having bad looks and a distorted body, is still better than many others with good looks.

424. ऊंचे पानी ना टिके, नीचे ही ठहराय।
     नीचा हो तो भरि पियै, ऊंचा प्यासा रह जाय॥

*Paani* (water) cannot stay on the hilltop, it flows and settles down at the low-lying base of the hill. So, if one lives (low) at the foothills, he will have plenty of water, while one living at the hilltop goes without water.

Purport: This verse focuses on one meaning of paani (water), while conveying a deeper parallel idea with a different meaning of paani (Godliness). Egoists will never get close to Godliness, while humble ones will.

425. गुरु बिन ग्यान न ऊपजे, गुरु बिन मिले ना मोश।
     गुरु बिन लिखे न सत्य को, गुरु बिन मिटे न दोष॥

Without a *Guru* (divine teacher), true knowledge cannot sprout; without a

*Guru*, one cannot achieve *moksha* (*Nirvana* or salvation); without a *Guru*, one cannot realize the ultimate "truth"; and without a *Guru*, evil within you cannot be removed.

426. भक्ति महल बहु ऊँच है, दूरहि ते दरसाय ।
जो कोई जन भक्ति करे, शोभा बरनि न जाय ॥

Devotion to God is like a towering monument that is visible from a distance. Whoever has devotion, his value in the world is indescribable.

427. नींद निशानी मौत की, ऊठ कबीरा जाग ।
और रसायन छोड़ के, नाम रसायन लाग ॥

O humans...Sleep [inaction, sluggishness] is the sign of ultimate demise. Wake up! Be active! Make use of the most effective spiritual formula, *the name of Lord Rama*...give up all other means. - <u>Kabir</u>

428. मागन मरण समान है, मति मांगो कोई भीख ।
मागन ते मरना भला, यह सतगुरू की सीख ॥

To plead for anything free is like death.
Do not beg. It is better to die than to
beg - this is the teaching of a real
*Guru.*

429. धन रहे न जोबन रहे, रहे न गॉव ना ठाम ।
    कबीरा जग मे जस रहे, कर दे किसी का काम ॥

Your wealth will go away, and so will
your youth, your home, and neighbors.
Only your *yash* (name and repute) will
remain, so one must work for the good
of others. - <u>Kabir</u>

430. खोद खाद धरती सहै, काट कूट बन राय ।
    कुटिल बचन साधू सहै, और से सहा न जाय ॥

Mother Earth endures indiscriminate
digging and disturbances, the forest
suffers brutal destruction and
elimination without protest. In the
same way, a *sadhu* (an enlightened
soul) tolerates abusive language which
no one can endure.

431. अछे के दिन पछे गये, हरि से किया ना हेत ।

अब पछताये होत का, जब चिड़िया चुग गयी खेत ॥

Time has flown by, but you did not remember God. Now what is the point of dwelling on it when it is already too late; just as it is too late for a farmer to guard his crop after birds and animals have already consumed it.

Purport - By the time one becomes old, it is too late to get onto the spiritual path. By that time, all of man's enemies (lust, greed, anger, ego and attachment) will have already vanquished his potential. - <u>Kabir</u>

432. हस्तस्य भूषणं दानं सत्यं कण्ठस्य भूषणम् ।
श्रोत्रस्य भूषणं शास्त्रं भूषणैः किं प्रयोजनम् ॥

The real ornament for the *hands* is "charity and helping others." The ornament for the *kantha* (neck, throat) is "speaking the truth."  Likewise, the ornament for the *ears* is "listening to scriptural knowledge." If a person is

endowed with these real ornaments,
what is the need for material
ornaments?

433. कर्मण्येवाधिकारस्ते मा फलेषु कदाचन ।
मा कर्मफलहेतुर्भूर्मा ते सङ्गोऽस्त्व कर्मणि ॥

You have a right to perform your work,
but never the right to choose its
outcome. You should never harbor the
pride of being the doer of your actions,
nor should you choose inaction. –
<u>Bhagavad-Gita</u>

434. जाको राखे साईया, मार सके ना कोय ।
बार न बाका कर सके, जो जग बैरी होय ॥

If God protects someone, no one can
kill him...no harm can be done even if
the whole world turns enemy.

435. रहिमन वे नर मर चुके, जो माँगन को जाय ।
उनसे पहले वो मरे, जिन मुख निकसत नाय ॥

Those who go for begging (or ask for
free stuff) are already dead. But even
before them, dead are those who

cannot utter from their mouths the
name of God. - <u>Rahim</u>

436. गोधन गजधन बाजिधन, और रतन की खान ।
जब आये संतोष धन, सब धन धूरि समान ॥

When "contentment" comes, all kinds
of wealth and heaps of jewels are like
dirt.

437. देनहार कोई और है, देवत है दिन रैन ।
लोग भरम हम पै करे, तासू नीचे नैन ॥

People think it is "me" who gives. In
reality, it is "somebody" else who gives
day and night. So, in all humility and
with the awareness of this knowledge, I
look down while giving. (*Rahim [1556-*
*1627 CE], a Moslem saint and a great*
*devotee of Krishna, answering a*
*question why he looked down while*
*giving alms*)

438. जिन खोजा तिन पाइयॉ, गहरे पानी पैठ ।
जो बौरा डूबन डरा, रहा किनारे बैठ ॥

He, who tried by diving deep, found the pearl (reward). He, who was afraid of drowning, kept sitting ashore and got nothing.

Purport: As long as the fear of suffering persists, you will not dare to explore the deeper dimensions of life.

439. दया धर्म का मूल है, पाप मूल अभिमान ।
तुलसी दया न छांड़िये, जब तक घट मे प्रान ॥

Compassion is the root of religion; ego is at the root of all sins. Do not let go of compassion as long as you have life in this body. - <u>Tulsi</u>

440. चाहन की चिंता गयी, मनवा बेपरवाह ।
जिनको कछु ना चाहिये, वो ही शहंशाह ॥

A king of kings is the one who has no wants for anything...no desires, no worries, and indifference to worldly things.

441. मानुष जनम दुलभ है, देह न बारंबार ।
तरूवर से फल छड़ पड़या, बहुरि न लागे डार ॥

The human body is not necessarily one begets often. To be born as human is difficult. If a fruit falls from the tree, it does not become part of the tree again.

442. आँते तीता दाँते नोन, पेट भरन को तीनो कोन ।
आँखैं पानी कानौं तेल, कहे घाघ वैदई गेल ॥

Spices for the digestive tract, salt for the teeth, three-fourth stomach-full of meal, water for the eyes and oil for the ears would eliminate the need of a doctor. [*There are very specific ways to use these simple preventive remedies, but no one should just accommodate these without proper understanding.*] - Ghaagh

443. पंथ दुर्गम तू अकेला क्या हुआ, मंजिले चूमेंगी कदम
संकल्प होना चाहिये ।

So what if the path ahead is difficult and you are alone? There must be a strong resolve...then only will success be at your feet.

444. हिम्मत है तेरे साथ, तो फिर साथ है भगवान ।
मेहनत ही तेरी इज्जत, मेहनत ही तेरी शान ॥

God is with you when you have
courage. Hard work is your honor; hard
work is your glory.

445. सत्य को जिसने न माना, उसको तो मिटना पड़ा है ।
बच गया तलवार से तो, फूल से कटना पड़ा है ॥

One who did not submit to the
authority of "truth" ended up meeting
his demise. If, by chance, he was able
to dodge the sword, he was cut into
pieces with flowers.

Purport: Those who are destined to
meet their demise for violating the law
of Nature cannot run away from the
consequences. If their demise does not
happen through obvious means, it will
happen through unexpected ones.

446. अति सर्वत्र वर्जति ।

Anything extreme is forbidden. -
Ancient Sanskrit proverb

447. अलसस्य कुतो विद्या, अविद्यस्य कुतो धनम् ।
अधनस्य कुतो मित्रम्, अमित्रस्य कुतः सुखम् ॥

For a lazy person, there is no education
(skill). Without education, there is no
wealth. Without wealth, there are no
friends. Without friends, there is no
happiness.

448. विदेशेषु धनं विद्या, व्यसनेषु धनं मतिः ।
परलोके धनं धर्मः, शीलं सर्वत्र वै धनम् ॥

In a foreign land, education (skills) is
wealth. At the time of difficulty, good
judgement is wealth. After death,
*dharma* (virtue, good Karma) is wealth.
*Sheel* (truthfulness, humility,
compassion, forgiveness, calmness.
good behavior and character) is wealth
everywhere.

449. पिंडे पिंडे मतिर्भिन्ना, कुंडे कुंडे नवं पयः ।
जातौ जातौ नवा चारा, नवा वाणी मुखे मुखे ॥

Every person has a uniquely different
mind; every source of water has a
different mineral content, every
culture/community has different ways

and lifestyle, and every person has uniquely different speech.

Purport: Do not generalize. Treat everyone uniquely.

450. अहिंसा परमो धर्मः, धर्म हिंसा तदैव च ।

Nonviolence is the greatest *dharma* (a set of eternal principles generally confused as *religion*, virtue, good Karma). But violence to protect *dharma* is even better. - <u>A couplet from the great epic Mahabharat</u>

451. आवत ही हरसे नहीं नयनन नहीं सनेह ।
तुलसी वहाँ न जाइये कंचन बरसे मेह ॥

If people are not happy upon your arrival and there is no affection in their eyes, do not go to such places even if it rains gold there. - <u>Tulsi</u>

452. करत-करत अभ्यास के, जड़मति होत सुजान ।
रसरी आवत-जात सो, सिल पर परत निशान ॥

Constant practice can sharpen even blunt minds. A rope, sliding back and forth, can even cut stone. - <u>Vrinda</u>

453. सरस्वती के भंडार की, बड़ी अपूरब बात ।
ज्यों ज्यों खरचे त्यों त्यों बढ़े, बिन खरचे घट जात ॥

As you spend (utilize) the treasure of intelligence, the greater it becomes. It disappears if not utilized. This is how the kingdom of Mother *Saraswati* (Goddess of intelligence) works. - <u>Vrinda</u>

454. मन जाणें सब बात, जाँणत ही औगुन करे ।
काहे की कुशलात, कर दीपक कूंवे पड़े ॥

The human mind is capable of understanding good and bad. Despite this, man commits bad deeds. There is no well-being of such people. Despite having light in hand, they fall into the darkness.

455. काक चेष्टा बकौ ध्यानं स्वान निद्रा तथैव च ।

A student should have the persistence
of a crow, the attention of a crane, and
the alertness of a dog when sleeping.
He should be an abstemious eater and
should not hesitate to leave his home
in pursuit of knowledge. These are five
characteristics of a sincere learner.

456. तन्मित्रं यत्र विश्वास:

Friendship is where trust is unshakable.

457. कठिन हमेशा कठिन नहीं होता है, और सरल तो कभी
भी सरल नहीं होता है।

What seems difficult is not always
difficult, and what seems easy is
certainly never easy.

www.ingramcontent.com/pod-product-compliance
Lightning Source LLC
Chambersburg PA
CBHW031235250726
48655CB00005B/1970